My Big

by Wiley Blevins

My city is big.

We have big buildings.

We have big streets.

Jongcheol Park/EyeEm/Getty Images

We have big statues.

Manamana/Shutterstock.com

We have big parks.

Medioimages/Photodisc/Getty Images

We have big homes.

My city is big!

Elenamiv/Shutterstock.com